#EXPERT EXCEL PROJECTS tweet
Book01

Taking Your Excel Project from Start to Finish Like an Expert

By Larry Moseley
Foreword by Ed Becmer

E-mail: info@thinkaha.com
20660 Stevens Creek Blvd., Suite 210,
Cupertino, CA 95014

Published by *THiNKaha®*, a Happy About® imprint
20660 Stevens Creek Blvd., Suite 210, Cupertino, CA 95014
http://thinkaha.com

First Printing: August 2011
Paperback ISBN: 978-1-61699-056-5 (1-61699-056-2)
eBook ISBN: 978-1-61699-057-2 (1-61699-057-0)
Place of Publication: Silicon Valley, California, USA
Paperback Library of Congress Number: 2011928351

Advance Praise

"A true 'go to' Excel project expert, Larry took our use of existing complex financial models to the next level. He was quick in deciphering current models, and modifying them to better reflect our business objectives. He also delivered superior decision support. Larry's book will be a 'must have' for all those who plan and implement an Excel project."

Elliott Josi, General Partner, MAPS Capital LLC and CEO, School Powers, LLC

"According to studies by the Big 4 accounting firms, 92% of large spreadsheets contain significant errors. Despite the high prevalence of these errors, finance departments seem to need the flexibility provided by Excel spreadsheets. I look forward to this book as a contribution to the quality of spreadsheet construction."

Steve Rabin, CPA, http://www.srabin.com

"Larry has helped me with existing and new Excel projects more than once. My clients and I have benefited from his mastery of Excel. I am glad that he is bringing his techniques to a larger audience by writing this book."

Mugdha Pendse, Consultant for Silicon Valley start-ups

Dedication

This book is dedicated to the individual contributors and finance managers who daily deal with the problems this book was designed to help alleviate.

Acknowledgments

Special thanks to my wife, Jan Moseley for her support, and indulgence while I was working on my manuscript and therefore glued to my monitor for hours on end. For the past 39 years of our marriage, she has always been supportive of my interest in computers and Excel programs.

Thanks to the many individuals and companies, I have worked with in the past. I always learn something new when working with these Excel projects. These individuals and companies have inspired me to write this book.

I would like to acknowledge Dave Osborne for his help in reviewing parts of the book and bringing to my attention additional ideas including SOX.

Thanks to Todd who sat with me in the early stages of my manuscript and reviewed my rough draft. He assisted me in solidifying my plan for the book and helped me overcome certain hurdles such as writer's block.

I would also like to thank Don Barber. He is a teacher, and gave me special insight into how the book would be read and interpreted by laypersons who were not Excel experts.

Thanks to Bob Beasley for taking the time to review some of the sections of my book.

Ken Shepard was helpful in pointing out some areas that I needed to improve on.

Greg Rose is currently studying for the CMA exam. A special thanks for taking the time to assist me.

Liz Tadman deserves special thanks for her assistance and patience in assisting me in the end game. I was walking where I had not walked before.

I especially want to thank Mitchell Levy for suggesting the idea and hanging with me as I worked my way through the development of this book.

Larry Moseley

Why Did I Write This Book?

I wanted to pass on the techniques I had developed to people I will not have a chance to help personally.

___

By providing a clear procedure to follow, I hope this book will increase your comfort level with developing Excel projects, and will also provide you with the guidance and confidence to successfully take on any project from beginning to end.

___

One of the more difficult tasks that individual contributors and finance managers must deal with is updating an Excel project when the developer has left the firm. I wrote this book with the hope that it could be used as a reference tool when navigating through this difficult time of transition.

___

There are many large Excel books that provide some of the concepts mentioned in this text, but those books are lengthy and difficult to wade through. This book provides a short concise reference book.

___

To provide Corporate Controllers and Chief Financial Officers (CFO) with a common operating procedure that their departments can use when developing or upgrading Excel projects.

___

I wanted to create a book that both experienced and less experienced Excel users would be able to follow and make use of on a regular basis.

___

Larry Moseley
Larry@LWMWEB.COM
http://WWW.LWMWEB.COM

Contents

Foreword

Larry Moseley's new book
EXPERT EXCEL PROJECTS tweet
provides insights and simple solutions
for complex and heavy Excel users
such as accountants, controllers, and
auditors. Now, there is a straightforward
reference book to help today's users plan,
implement, and manage their day-to-day
use of Excel spreadsheets.

Ed Becmer,
CPA, CTP-D
Partner, CFOs2GO

Section 1

What to Do Before You Start

Before starting a project, you need to determine what you want to accomplish, your data source, and what you want to present and to whom. Without a clear road map, your project may not end when and where you hoped it would. Road maps allow you to articulate your objectives and the strategies you shall use in reaching these goals, so take the time to map out your project before you begin!

1

When starting a new Excel project it pays to plan ahead. Careful pre-planning can eliminate many common errors.

2

Part of the starting process is determining what you want to accomplish and what steps you need to take.

3

Ask yourself this question. Is your project going to be used by one person (yourself) or will multiple people be using it?

4

Changes are inevitable. Planning for future maintenance will assist you or others in making those changes.

5

Know your data and how it will be input. Is your data coming from an outside source and/or being input by the user?

6

When you know where your data will be coming from, determine how you will receive it, and how you will upload and store this data.

7

To keep your project on track, you should write your plan to include periodic milestones. This will help you to monitor your progress.

8

It is always easier to document your work as you go rather than to go back later and figure out what you did and why.

9

Plan the use of colors carefully. Use colors only to highlight special sections like data input areas.

10

Use a logical layout plan for the workbook tabs. Put common numbers or constants on an input page and link to other worksheets.

11

In your plan, include the following: a final summation page(s) designed for viewing first, an input tab, and then subsidiary worksheets.

12

If your worksheets are for viewing, design the layout for easy viewing.

13

You may need to insert additional rows or columns in the future. Design your plan to facilitate this.

14

When planning a monthly annual forecast, decide how the user will be able to add the next year by a simple copy paste.

15

The requirements for performance or ease of use are different. Decide what is most important and develop with that in mind.

16

If you know how to use Excel macros, they can enhance the automation of special functions.

17

Learn how to document your macros using the Visual Basic Editor.

18

To speed up the process of importing outside data an Excel macro may be used. You will also be able to add automatic error checking.

19

Do not over use macros. Use macros only when normal Excel functions are not adequate.

20

If using VBA mathematical functions, confirm that they are calculating the way you want them to. Not all functions are equal.

21

Whether you are public or private, work with your auditors or in-house SOX group about being in conformance with SOX section 404.

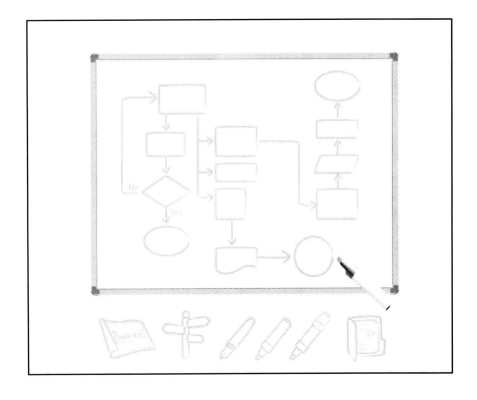

Section II

How to Get Where You Want to Go

When you begin a new project, you need to "Storyboard" the steps you are going to take to get from the data to the finished product. The creation of a storyboard requires that you draw a diagram that will assist you in determining how many sections are required for your spreadsheet, and what formulas you will need. Spend time and effort in creating a detailed, well thought out storyboard, because this will help you later on down the road when you begin working on your Excel project.

22

Your plan must be written down. A storyboard or flowchart should be a key component in the creation process.

23

Without a detailed plan, you may not end up where you wanted to be, and you may lack accurate data.

24

The first step should be to determine your final output. Then you will know what data you will need.

25

Determine what data will need to be downloaded from an outside source, what data will be input by a user, and what data must be calculated.

26

When using external data, the best way to begin is to review your Vendor's documentation.

27

If working with external data, coordinate with IT to develop a plan for how the data will be downloaded.

28

Ensure that the data comes from the ERP system in the same format each time. An added or relocated column will destroy your work.

29

Use test totals to ensure the data you download has the same totals as your ERP systems download.

30

Design your project with certain values in mind. Ease of data input and viewing accessibility are important to users.

31

Group input on worksheets in the same location. Then link to it for calculations. This will greatly simplify data input and validation.

32

Build sections and
worksheets one-step at
a time. Test each section
or worksheet prior to
continuing.

33

Make sure you understand the Excel functions you will be using and how best to optimize them.

34

Excel calculates from the top to the bottom and left to right. Plan your headings across the top and data down the rows.

35

Put as many variables and constants on a single worksheet as possible. This simplifies input and control.

36

Use the footer to place the file name and date (time while developing) at the bottom of all printouts.

37

Backing up your data is important, but you need to save different versions as you make changes.

38

Do more than simply backing up your files periodically. Save the file with a different version number.

39

Save new versions every time you are going to make major changes or additions.

40

Sequentially numbered backups allow you to retrace your steps one at a time to locate where you made an error more easily.

41

Avoid chain linking. When linking to an input or constant, always link to the same original source.

42

Try to avoid linking to multiple workbooks.

43

If appropriate, when linking to multiple workbooks, consider forcing automatic updating in Excel when your workbook is opened.

44

As you proceed, keep future changes and maintenance needs in mind. Proper steps now will save time and frustration later.

45

Try to keep all linked workbooks in the same folder. This will help eliminate broken links in the future.

46

Do not place subordinate calculations between rows or columns of contiguous formulas or data.

47

Standardize your format when using separate worksheets to calculate common types of data.

48

Use standardized worksheets within more complicated workbooks like multiple departments, but leave room for special situations.

49

To assist in changes or updates, standardize departmental forecasts or other common sections.

50

Do not over use complex
functions and formulas unless
necessary. Try breaking them into
separate calculations.

51

To make your job easier in the future,
document any changes and additions
as you progress with your project.

52

Break complex formulas into their constituent parts and note the flow of logic. Include this in your documentation for future reference.

53

You need to test your work at intermediate steps. It is easier to make corrections now, than later when things are more complicated.

54

If you are experienced in VBA use _Excel User forms_ to facilitate data input.

55

Excel _Dynamic Tables_ may simplify the use of data.

56

Use _Input Message_ from the _Data Validation_ menu, or _Comments_ to inform your users of needed information.

57

The *Input Message* does not display, unless the cell is selected. When the cell is selected, it can specify the proper data to be input.

58

Use *Conditional Formatting* in combination with the input message to ease data input and help eliminate incorrect information.

59

Reserve Comments for noting non-critical changes in the worksheet design or formulas.

60

Follow these guidelines; it is easier to make corrections as you go. Corrections will become more complicated as your project proceeds.

Section III

Working with Formulas and Formatting

In various studies in which spreadsheets were reviewed, a significant number of them contained errors in the use of functions as well as modeling errors.[1] Prevent these common mistakes by stablishing proper guidelines and following the rules set forth in those guidelines. Adhering to a set procedural plan will help you to create an effective and efficient spreadsheet project. Taking the time to plan ahead will also assist you in remembering the specific details of a project, such as what the spreadsheet was for and why it was created. The accessibility of this information will be very useful if needed weeks, months, or years from now.

---

1. Appendix C: Spreadsheet Considerations

61

Test your formulas and use of functions separately using known data and results.

62

When designing more complicated formulas, write them as a text statement first.

63

Write and test each section of a complex formula separately before combining the sections into the final formula.

64

Testing separate sections of a complex formula will increase efficiency and save enough time to allow for writing documentation.

65

Create your formulas with consistency.
A1+B1+C1+D1 not A1+D1+C1+B1.

66

Input data only once. Use direct links
when the data needs will be used in
multiple formulas.

67

Excel uses calculation preference, but for clear viewing and debugging, always separate distinct operations with parentheses.

68

To eliminate misunderstandings, when viewing the numbers presented in the future, always format them.

69

Understand and use *Relative* and *Absolute* references to enhance the ability to copy and paste.

70

When using functions use the Excel wizard and follow the notes for each input.

71

Learn to use the *Auditing Tool Bar* in Excel. To evaluate a complex formula, use the *Evaluate Formula* tool.

72

Try using the *Error Checking* tool in the *Formula Toolbar* to find potential errors.

73

When reviewing formulas, use the *Trace Precedents* tool to trace dependent relationships and to clarify the formula.

74

Use the *Watch Window* to determine how changes in constants affect the various equations.

75

Use _Pivot Tables_ and _Array Formulas_ sparingly, as they require greater storage and memory usage.

76

Test raw data and confirm that the _Pivot Table_ displays the correct totals.

77

Use the *SUMIF()* function to develop the totals from the raw data to check your data with some of your Pivot Table totals.

78

Use Excel's *Data Validation* tools in the data menu to validate user input.

79

When summing columns and rows, always cross-foot the totals to ensure accuracy.

80

If you see an error message like #DIV/0!, #N/A, #REF!, etc. do not ignore them. Fixing these errors will make your results more reliable.

81

Try using Dynamic Ranges when your imported data fluctuates in length.

82

Conditional Formatting is a powerful tool with a wide range of formatting possibilities that should be used for powerful visual effects.

Section IV

Important Mid Game Considerations

You are almost there. No project goes perfectly from start to finish. If you follow your plan, these guidelines, and pay close attention to potential issues and concerns, you can highlight problems early, when they are still easily fixable.

83

Review your plan and confirm you are following it. If you need to take a different direction, update your documentation.

84

Use _range names_ sparingly. Too many range names will cause confusion.

85

Learn the difference on how to use _specific_ (worksheet) or _global_ (workbook) scope in range names.

86

When potential inputs are static, use Excel's various *Form Controls* such as *Drop Down Boxes* and *Spin Buttons*.

87

To prevent future headaches, when wanting to hide rows or columns, use the *Group/Ungroup* buttons not the hide rows and columns function.

88

Using a blank row as the terminus for all Sums will eliminate a future insertion at the bottom that is not included in the _SUM()_.

89

Always format your numbers visually, to confirm that the number you thought was in thousands is indeed in thousands.

90

Learn how to use the formula display mode on the Audit Tool Bar. This provides for a visual review of your formulas for consistency.

91

Do not hard code numbers when included in a range of common formulas.

92

Do not place a unique formula within a range of common formulas unless it is necessary. Use _Excel Comments_ to note the unique formula.

93

Placing dates and other common numbers in one location and then linking to this location will ensure they change wherever they are used.

94

Providing error checks in your work with text based error messages will increase the chance that they will be noticed.

95

Text based error codes can be included in an *IF Statement*. This is an example. =IF(B5<>C5,"Error","")

96

When summing down rows and across columns, provide a separate check total that confirms these totals are consistent.

97

If cents are unimportant in your check totals, use the round function to eliminate minute check errors.

98

To simplify multiple sums, consider using Excel's _Sumproduct Function_.

99

When printing or viewing the same data differently, try using custom views.

100

When including a calculated number within a text string, use the _Text_ and _Concatenate_ functions to make dynamic changes.

101

When printing or viewing multiple pages, fix the titles to reprint on each page or view.

102

Experiment with the choices above to find what best fits your project's purpose. Your choices will affect the effectiveness of the project.

Section V

What to Do When You Think You Are Done

The real work begins when you think you are done. You need to confirm your logic and ensure that what you present is a true reflection of the data. Studies have found that a significant number of the workbooks reviewed had output that was misinterpreted.[2] Honest mistakes happen, but these misinterpretations can be easily caught and fixed by always checking your work.

---

2. Appendix C: Spreadsheet Considerstions

103

Highlight input cells or areas with a distinctive color to facilitate data input.

104

To prevent write-over's and to allow tabbing for input, unlock input cells for each worksheet and then protect it.

105

Return to your original flow charts
and concepts and confirm that you
have included all of the items you
planned to incorporate.

106

If you are importing data, double-check
your work to ensure that the imported
data is always in the same format.

107

Avoid spreadsheet creep.
In your final documentation,
provide for changes, so they
can be made intelligently
in the future.

108

You should have been updating your documentation as you went. Now complete your documentation and finalize it.

109

Use 0 (zero) inputs to verify that calculations that should go to 0 do. Then test the results with numbers like 100k, 200k, and 300k.

110

Double-check your views for clarity. If the viewer sees things differently than you intended, this can cause unfavorable interpretations.

111

Have an experienced associate work with your Excel project and give you feedback on the ease of use and the logic.

112

Have a less experienced associate review your Excel project for ease of input and correctness of presented data.

113

Perform an audit to rule out potential errors in the original project. Where possible, compare and validate the differences that you find.

114

Save a historical version in another location, for future reference.

115

Implement version control for ongoing use. Whether there are multiple users or one, everyone must be working on the same version.

116

Schedule periodic reviews to confirm the applicability of the output with the purpose stated in the documentation.

117

Congratulate yourself, because you have *taken your Excel project from start to finish like an expert!*

Section VI

How to Decipher and Change Someone Else's Excel Project

Many times, you may need to work with an Excel project that someone else developed, and the original developer may no longer be available to answer and explain questions that arise. Many of the items addressed in the first five sections of this book are applicable when beginning work on a new Excel project, but there are different techniques that must be utilized in this type of situation. With existing projects, you must think like a detective. A good detective always gathers information meticulously, confirming its place in the investigation before moving on.

118

Save your own historical copy for future reference. This can be invaluable when you run into problems while making changes.

119

Your first step should be a visual review of the main display pages. Look for obvious errors like missing or illogical numbers and formulas.

120

Study the data used for the spreadsheet's composition. Determine whether it is user input, obtained from an outside source, or both.

121

Start your documentation by creating a flowchart. Illustrate the flow of data and logic through the project before making any changes.

122

Always document as you go. Use screen prints and short descriptions as a part of your review of the project.

123

Check for existing external
connections and verify
their validity.

124

Do not make snap judgments as to the validity of the old project or the logic used. Complete your analysis before considering changes.

125

Before making changes to formulas, decide if the layout of the formula was necessary and needs to remain as a part of the project.

126

If a formula is a result of spreadsheet creep, track its use both as a dependant and as a precedent to other calculations before making changes.

127

Begin your detailed analysis at the final output and proceed working backwards. You should not miss steps doing your analysis this way.

128

Use the *Auditing Tool* on the *Formulas Ribbon* to follow the logic of the calculations. Check for links to empty cells or erroneous data.

129

Carefully check for hidden rows or columns. Use the *Group* function to hide rows or columns from view.

130

If check or auditing calculations are not present, add them to confirm totals, debit credit conformity, and data integrity.

131

Go to Section II and follow the guidelines to prepare your changes in a well thought out, carefully planned manner.

132

Confer with your manager or client to confirm that your plan will meet or exceed the needs of the company.

133

Read (or review) the steps outlined in Sections III and IV. Follow these steps just as you would with a new project.

134

Similar to a new project, sequentially numbered backups allow you to retrace each step to find where you made an error more easily.

135

Periodically checking the effects of your changes in other worksheets will save you from wasted hours of work if errors are later found.

136

Always check every worksheet after making major changes to confirm that the changes you made did not cause errors elsewhere.

137

To improve your reconstruction when consolidating worksheets, do not delete eliminated worksheets until you have completed your work.

138

Periodically check your current calculations with the original workbooks' calculations where they are accurate.

139

Periodically stop and test the entire project with new data and confirm everything flows properly.

140

Audit the current applicability of the final output and follow the steps in Section V.

Appendix A: Postscript

I want to thank you for buying this book, I know it will help you in producing better Excel projects.

In deciding what to include in this book I have leaned heavily on my 30 years of experience working with and revamping other people's projects. The tweets are a combination of general and specific recommendations.s

You will notice several items mentioned in more than one section (i.e. documentation and sequential backups). I highlight and stress these items because of the importance I place on them for a successful conclusion to your project.

You will hear different opinions about how to do an Excel project. There is always another way in Excel. That is why it is so widely used. The procedures I have outlined are not overly conservative; however, you may need to bend the procedure in special situations to accommodate your specific needs.

My original manuscript had many ideas that I later deleted. Some of the people who reviewed this book mentioned other excellent concepts that could have been included. I had to use my experience in picking the most useful ideas while also managing to keep the book at a reasonable length. Some of the decisions were difficult, but like a movie director, I needed to leave some ideas on the cutting room floor.

Taking Your Excel Project from Start to Finish Like an Expert

Appendix B: Additional Information

Some of the specific recommendations may be new to some users. I will place some white papers on my website that purchasers of the book may use to enhance their Project abilities. These white papers will be available on my website at http://www.lwmweb.com/planning/.

Some of those items will be:

- Documentation
- VBA
- Error checking
- Sequential numbers
- Relative and Absolute numbers
- Auditing tool bar
- Error codes
- Concatenating
- Data validation

Appendix C: Spreadsheet Considerations

Many studies confirm the high error rate in existing spreadsheets used in corporate America. My experience with existing Excel projects validates this problem. Doing a Google search brings up these studies and horror stories. However, most of the links attempt to sell you software or subscriptions to their website. I have selected several of the better links and included them here.

Link to full text and pull down link to pdf.
http://www.heinz.cmu.edu/faculty-and-research/research/research-details/index.aspx?rid=272

This is a long article but the various charts will be very informative.
http://panko.shidler.hawaii.edu/ssr/Mypapers/whatknow.htm

PWC article on SOX 404 (this is a direct link to the PDF):
http://www.auditsoftware.net/community/excel/PwCwpSpreadsheetsSection404Sarbox.pdf

Taking Your Excel Project from Start to Finish Like an Expert

About the Author

Larry has maintained a stellar 35-year track record working as a finance executive in corporate America. He has applied his financial acumen in a range of corporate environments, ranging from business startups to large corporations. Over the years, Larry has developed several complex projects using Excel and has also reviewed and simplified existing projects. His experience is evident in the knowledge that he sets forth in this book.

Larry was introduced to spreadsheets when the IBM PC was released. Filling a need at local computer stores, he learned the spreadsheets then available for the IBM PC and taught their spreadsheet classes. He has continued teaching and provides "hands-on" Excel classes for companies and organizations.

Larry has used spreadsheets as an intricate part of his toolbox and has used Excel in all of his business consulting. At one time or another, he has used most of Excel's functioning capabilities, including VBA (Visual Basic for Applications).

Many studies have discussed the high error rate prevalent in existing spreadsheets used throughout corporate America. Larry's experiences improving existing Excel projects have confirmed the validity of these studies and their causes. As he works with existing projects, Larry is constantly developing his techniques of investigation and improvement.

Other Books in the THiNKaha Series

The THiNKaha book series is for thinking adults who lack the time or desire to read long books, but want to improve themselves with knowledge of the most up-to-date subjects. THiNKaha is a leader in timely, cutting-edge books and mobile applications from relevant experts that provide valuable information in a fun, Twitter-brief format for a fast-paced world.

They are available online at http://thinkaha.com or at other online and physical bookstores.

1. *#BOOK TITLE tweet Book01:* 140 Bite-Sized Ideas for Compelling Article, Book, and Event Titles by Roger C. Parker

2. *#BUSINESS SAVVY PM tweet Book01:* Project Management Mindsets, Skills, and Tools for Generating Successful Business Results by Cinda Voegtli

3. *#COACHING tweet Book01:* 140 Bite-Sized Insights On Making A Difference Through Executive Coaching by Sterling Lanier

4. *#CONTENT MARKETING tweet Book01:* 140 Bite-Sized Ideas to Create and Market Compelling Content by Ambal Balakrishnan

5. *#CORPORATE CULTURE tweet Book01:* 140 Bite-Sized Ideas to Help You Create a High Performing, Values Aligned Workplace that Employees LOVE by S. Chris Edmonds

6. *#CROWDSOURCING tweet Book01:* 140 Bite-Sized Ideas to Leverage the Wisdom of the Crowd by Kiruba Shankar and Mitchell Levy

7. *#DEATHtweet Book01:* A Well-Lived Life through 140 Perspectives on Death and Its Teachings by Timothy Tosta

8. *#DEATH tweet Book02:* 140 Perspectives on Being a Supportive Witness to the End of Life by Timothy Tosta

9. *#DIVERSITYtweet Book01:* Embracing the Growing Diversity in Our World by Deepika Bajaj

10. *#DREAMtweet Book01:* Inspirational Nuggets of Wisdom from a Rock and Roll Guru to Help You Live Your Dreams by Joe Heuer

11. *#ENTRYLEVELtweet Book01:* Taking Your Career from Classroom to Cubicle by Heather R. Huhman

12. *#ENTRY LEVEL tweet Book02:* Inspiration for New Professionals by Christine Ruff and Lori Ruff

13. *#EXPERT EXCEL PROJECTS tweet:* Taking Your Excel Project From Start To Finish Like An Expert by Larry Moseley

14. *#IT OPERATIONS MANAGEMENT tweet Book01:* Managing Your IT Infrastructure in The Age of Complexity by Peter Spielvogel, Jon Haworth, Sonja Hickey

15. *#JOBSEARCHtweet Book01:* 140 Job Search Nuggets for Managing Your Career and Landing Your Dream Job by Barbara Safani

16. *#LEADERSHIPtweet Book01:* 140 Bite-Sized Ideas to Help You Become the Leader You Were Born to Be by Kevin Eikenberry

17. *#LEADS to SALES tweet Book01:* Creating Qualified Business Leads in the 21st Century by Jim McAvoy

18. *#LEAN SIX SIGMA tweet Book01:* Business Process Excellence for the Millennium by Dr. Shree R. Nanguneri

19. *#LEAN STARTUP tweet Book01:* 140 Insights for Building a Lean Startup! by Seymour Duncker

20. *#MILLENNIALtweet Book01:* 140 Bite-Sized Ideas for Managing the Millennials by Alexandra Levit

21. *#MOJOtweet:* 140 Bite-Sized Ideas on How to Get and Keep Your Mojo by Marshall Goldsmith

22. *#MY BRAND tweet Book01:* A Practical Approach to Building Your Personal Brand - 140 Characters at a Time by Laura Lowell

23. *#OPEN TEXTBOOK tweet Book01:* Driving the Awareness and Adoption of Open Textbooks by Sharyn Fitzpatrick

24. *#PARTNER tweet Book01:* 140 Bite-Sized Ideas for Succeeding in Your Partnerships by Chaitra Vedullapalli

THiNK Continuity™ Training/Learning Program

THiNK Continuity™ delivers high-quality, cost-effective continuous learning in easy-to-understand, worthwhile, and digestible chunks. Fifteen minutes with a *THiNKaha*® book will allow the reader to have one or more "aha" moments. An hour and a half monthly with a THiNK Continuity program will allow the learner to have an opportunity to truly digest the topic being covered.

Offered online and/or in person, these engaging programs feature gurus (ours and yours) on such relevant topics as Leadership, Management, Sales, Marketing, Work-Life Balance, Project Management, Social Media and Networking, Presentation Skills, and other topics of your choosing. The "learning" audience, whether it is clients, employees or partners, can now experience high-quality learning that will enhance your brand value and empower your company as a thought leader. This program fits a real need where time and the high cost of developing custom content are no longer an option for every organization.

Just **THiNK**...

- **C**ontinuous Employee/Client/Prospect Learning
- **O**ngoing Thought Leadership Development
- **N**otable Experts Presenting on Relevant Topics
- **T**ime Your Attendees Can Afford – 15 min. to 2 hrs/mth
- **I**nformation Delivered in Digestible Chunks
- **N**ame the Topic – We Help You Provide Expert Best Practices
- **U**nderstand and Implement the Takeaways
- **I**nternal Expertise Shared Externally
- **T**raining/Prospecting Cost Decreases, Effectiveness Increases
- **Y**ou Win, They Win!